THE VERY VERY VERY VERY LONG DOG

H. E. TODD

ILLUSTRATED BY VAL BIRO

CORGI CAROUSEL

This is a story about a dog. When he was a puppy he was just a little, soft lump with big silky ears and they called him "Humph" (short for Humphrey) — and still do most of the time.

Then he grew older and rather longer and they sometimes called him "Humphalumph".

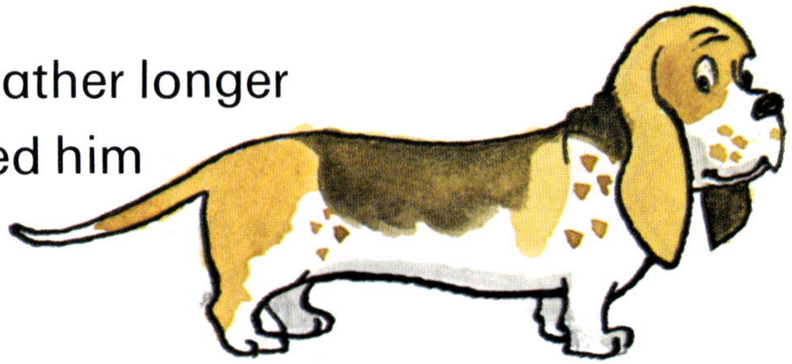

Then, quite suddenly, and for a few days only, he became a very, very, very long dog indeed, and they gave him an extra "Lumph" and started calling him "Humphalumphalumph".

Perhaps you wonder how all this happened so suddenly and for a few days only? Well — it's a long story, and here it is — but to save time and space I will just call him "Humph" (short for Humphrey) as I tell it.

One day not long ago, when he was just rather a long dog, his mistress took Humph shopping with her. They walked through the streets and over the main crossroads until they reached a large store and went inside.

Looking at things inside the store was all very interesting for his mistress but not much fun for Humph because all he could see was

Then she wanted to buy something on the first floor and they went to the escalator. She was still thinking about her shopping and failed to read the notice at the bottom which clearly said "DOGS MUST BE CARRIED ON THE ESCALATOR".

Humph had never seen an escalator before and he was suspicious. He put his front paws on the moving staircase and his mistress stepped on it herself. But he had forgotten about his back legs and was too frightened to move them. His mistress was so interested in the display of clothes on the way up that she did not notice that Humph was still standing at the bottom of the escalator and his front legs were being pulled

DOGS MUST BE
CARRIED ON THE
ESCALATOR

Then she glanced down at him and SCREAMED! A customer at the bottom of the escalator heard her scream and saw what was happening. He lifted Humph's back legs on to the moving staircase, but it was too late. Humph did not shoot back to his old shape like a piece of elastic. His front legs were half-way up and his back legs were still far below and he

By the time she reached the first floor his mistress was in a frightful state and the Floor Manager had to give her a glass of water and an aspirin. But it was really Humph who needed attention.

Another customer had a bright idea. He held Humph's front paws when they reached the top of the stairs hoping that the escalator would push his back legs and close him up like a telescope. But it did not work. As the escalator rose Humph was pushed

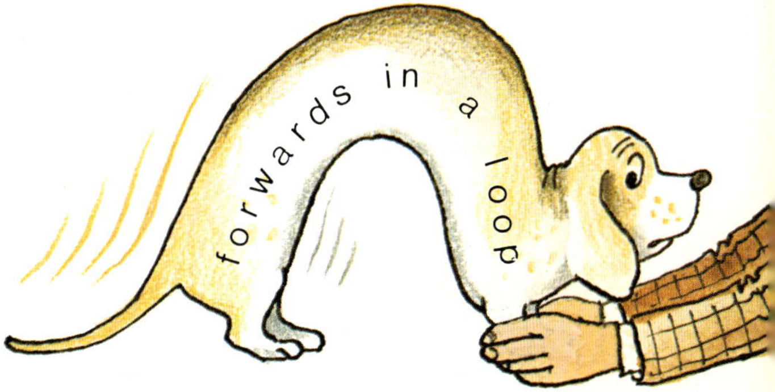

Then they tried the other way round. Humph ran as fast as he could down the upwards escalator while the customer held his back legs. But that did not work either. When he stopped running Humph was pushed

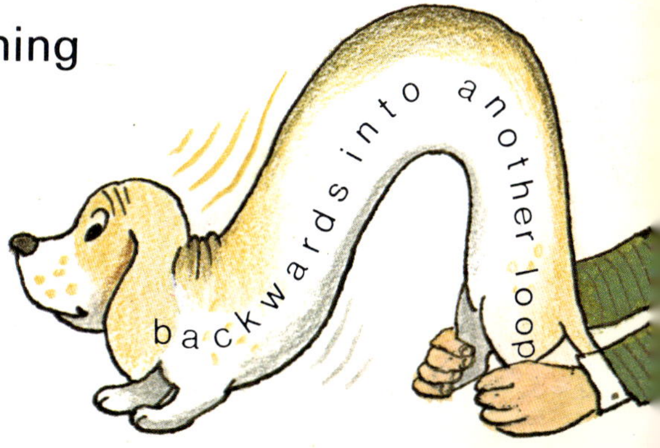

His mistress was now feeling better and beginning to realise that Humph was stuck in his new long shape. And Humph was beginning to enjoy his new shape because people took much more notice of him. For instance, when his mistress went to a counter to buy something, the lady assistant was amazed to see his

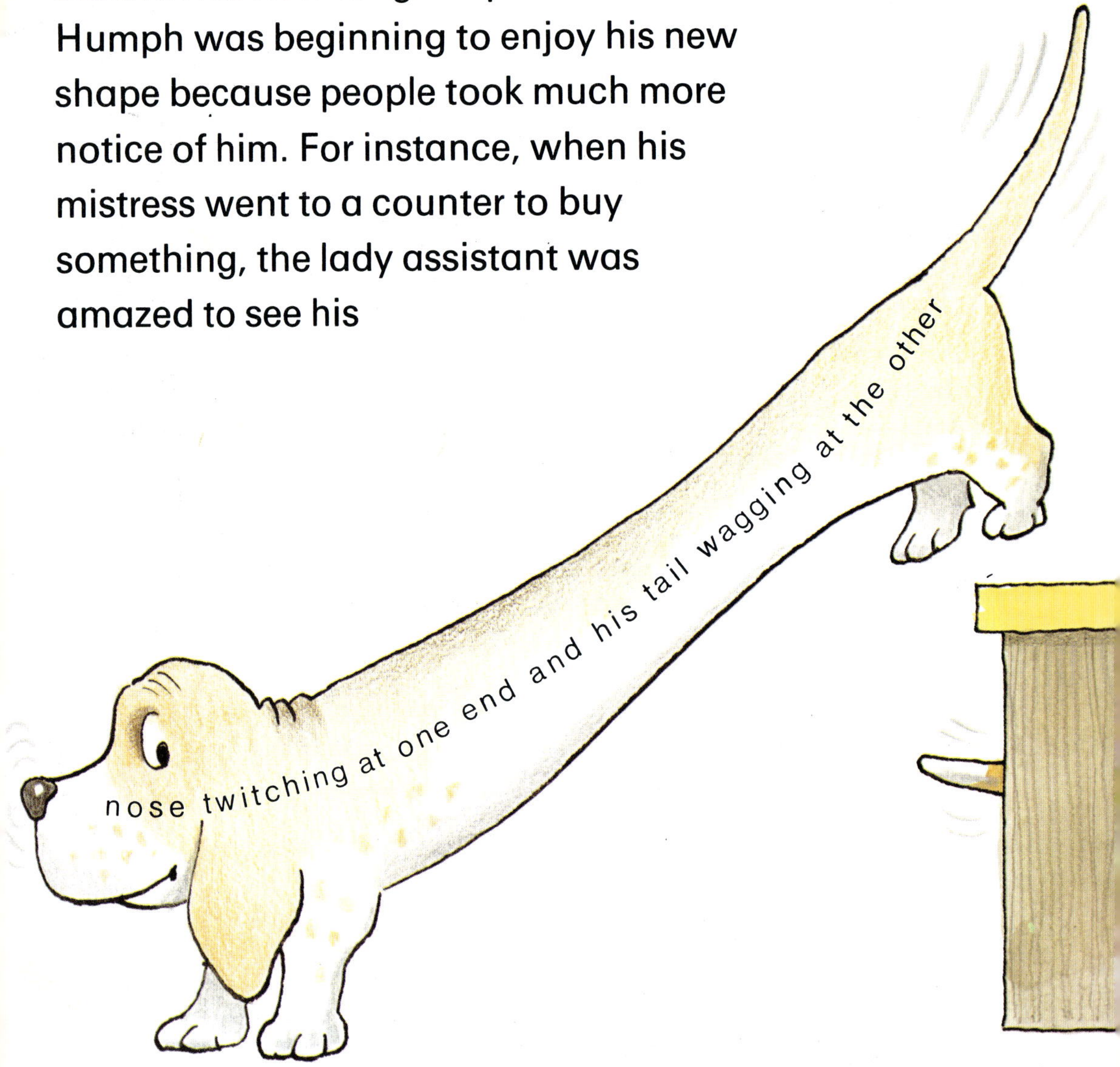

Then, on the way out of the store, the Ground Floor Manager and his Chief Assistant had to hold open the swing doors

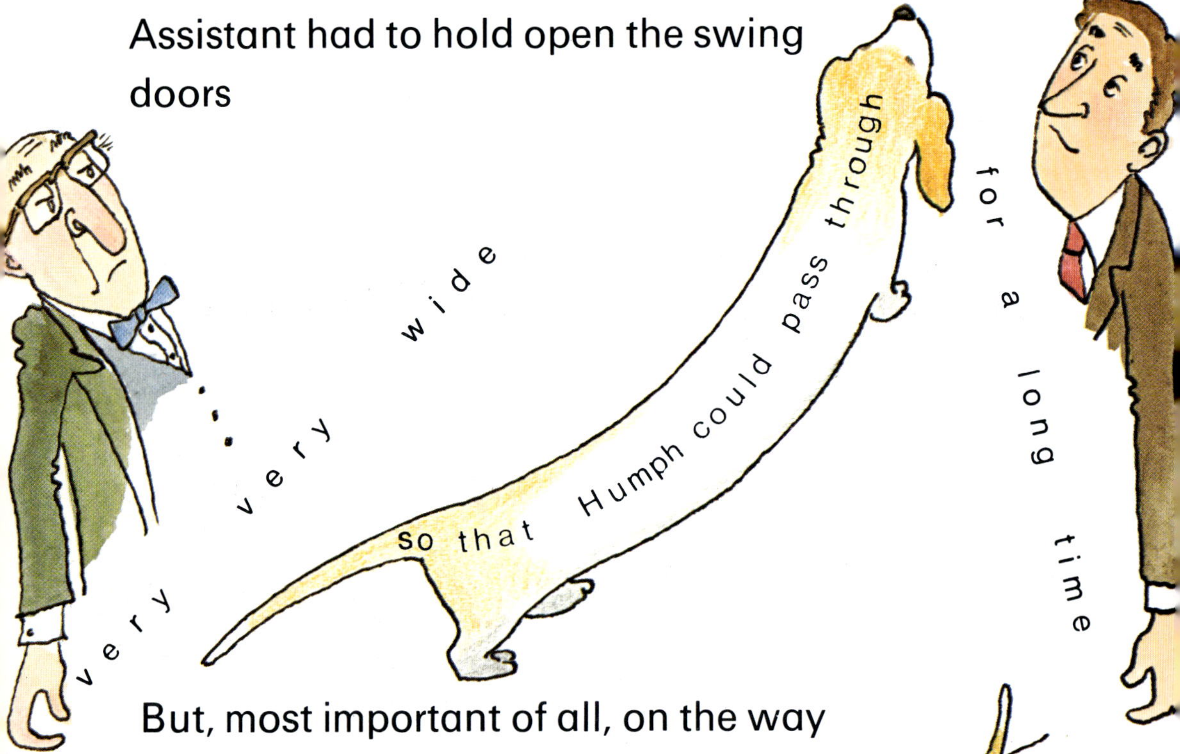

. . . very very very wide so that Humph could pass through for a long time

But, most important of all, on the way home the big policeman at the main crossroads had to hold up the traffic

all four ways just for Humph

PX

After dinner (which took a long time to go down), Humph thought he would run to the school nearby and show himself to the children. They were delighted with him and played all sorts of games.

First, he stood nose to tail and they danced round him singing

Then he made an arch and they played

Then he just lay down on his back, right across the playground with his paws in the air and they played

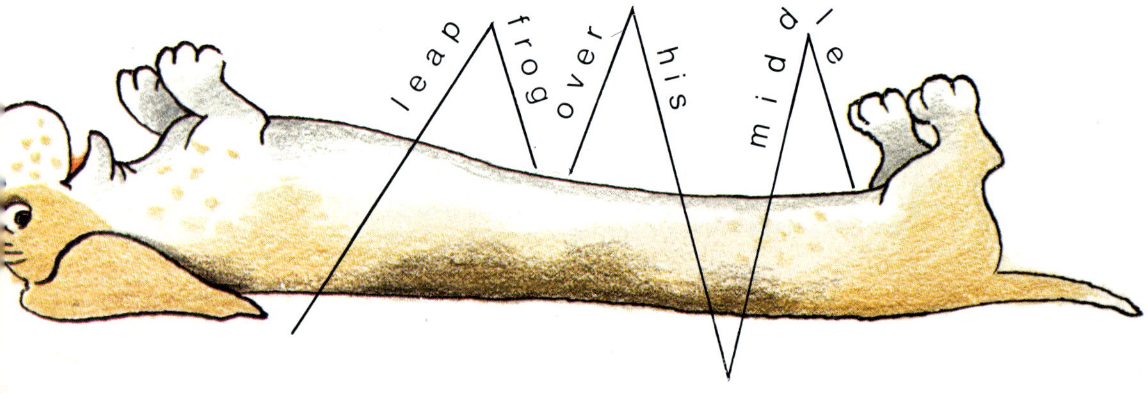

When school was over Humph felt tired after such an exciting day and his mistress found him a big basket in which to sleep. It was lovely and snug because he

In the middle of the night a very exciting thing happened. Humph heard a noise outside and jumped out of his basket.

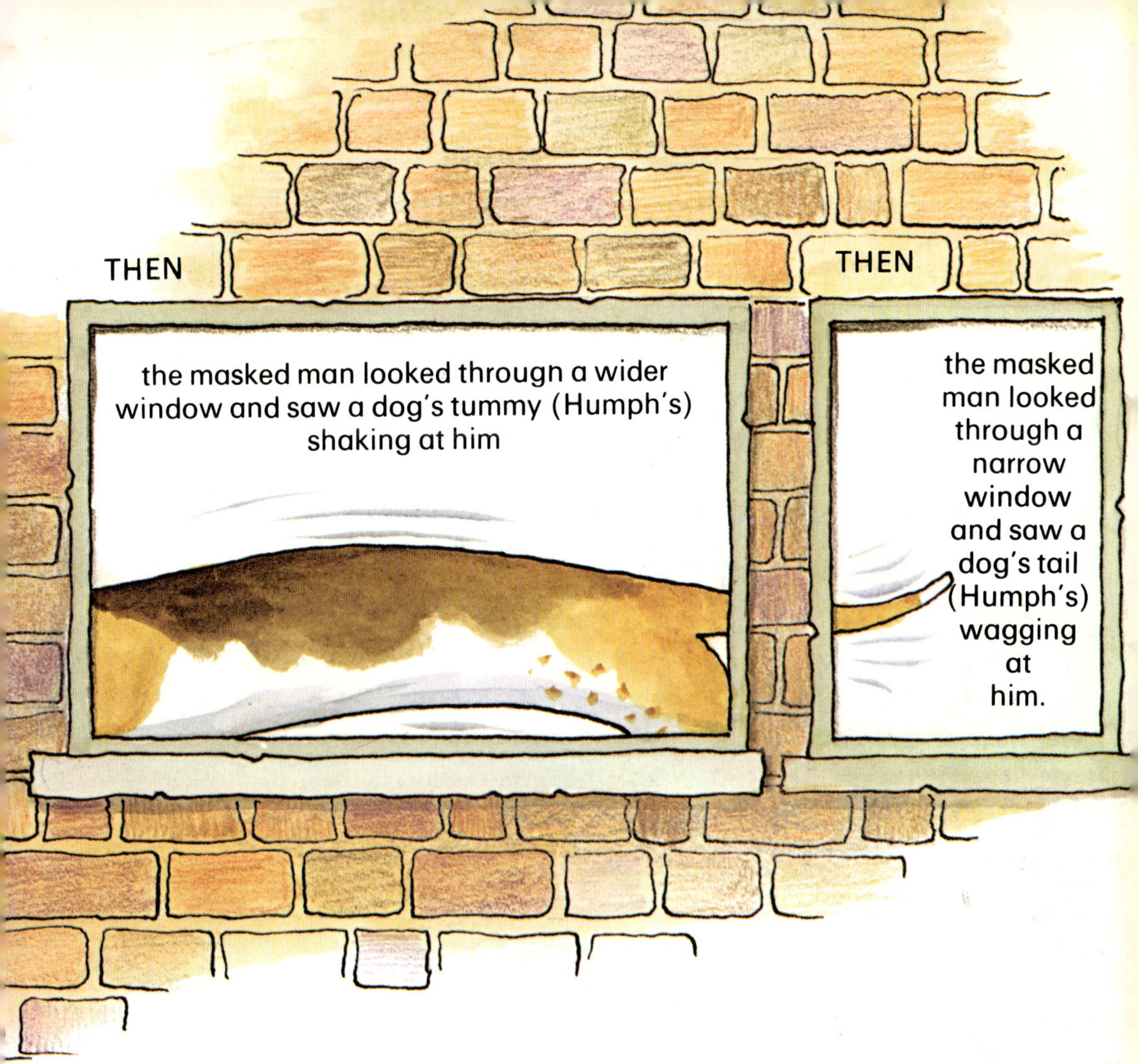

"Oh dear," said the masked man to himself. "There are THREE dogs in this house—one in each window. I must get away as quickly as I can."

And when his mistress heard the barking, ran downstairs, and saw the man climbing over the wall, she told Humph that he was a very, very, very brave dog as well as being a very, very, very long one.

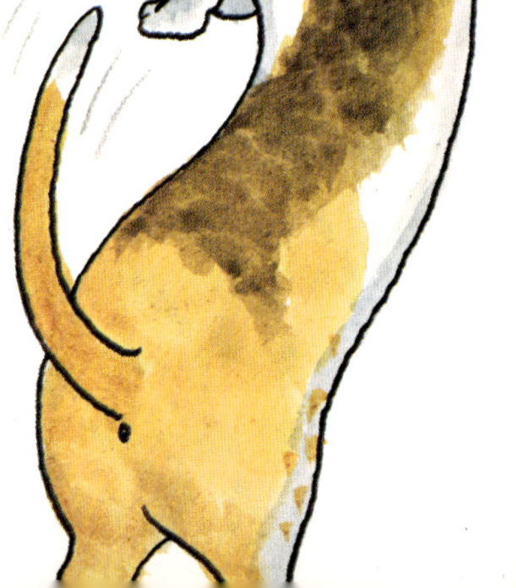

But the most exciting things of all happened afterwards. Humph's mistress reported what had happened to the police, and they must have told the newspaper people about it, for that evening an article appeared in print about brave Humph which spread over

PAGE 1

PAGE 2

AND

PAGE 3

And that wasn't all. The paper came to the notice of the television people, and they produced a programme about Humph which appeared in THREE episodes

AND

The end bit
on
WEDNESDAY

By Thursday Humph was beginning to feel tired of being so famous because people seemed to be laughing at him most of the time, and that made him feel ridiculous. But during that morning something happened which suddenly brought everything back to normal. When he woke up he unwound and stretched himself (which took a long, long time), and after breakfast, to get away from it all, he went to see his old friend, the lady cat next door.

One of her kittens was stranded up on the branch of a tree and too frightened to come down. She asked Humph to help her with the rescue. All Humph had to do was run up the trunk of the tree with his front legs and then sit on his back legs, and the kitten was able to

All the other kittens thought that it looked great fun, and they asked Humph to stay there so that one after the other they could

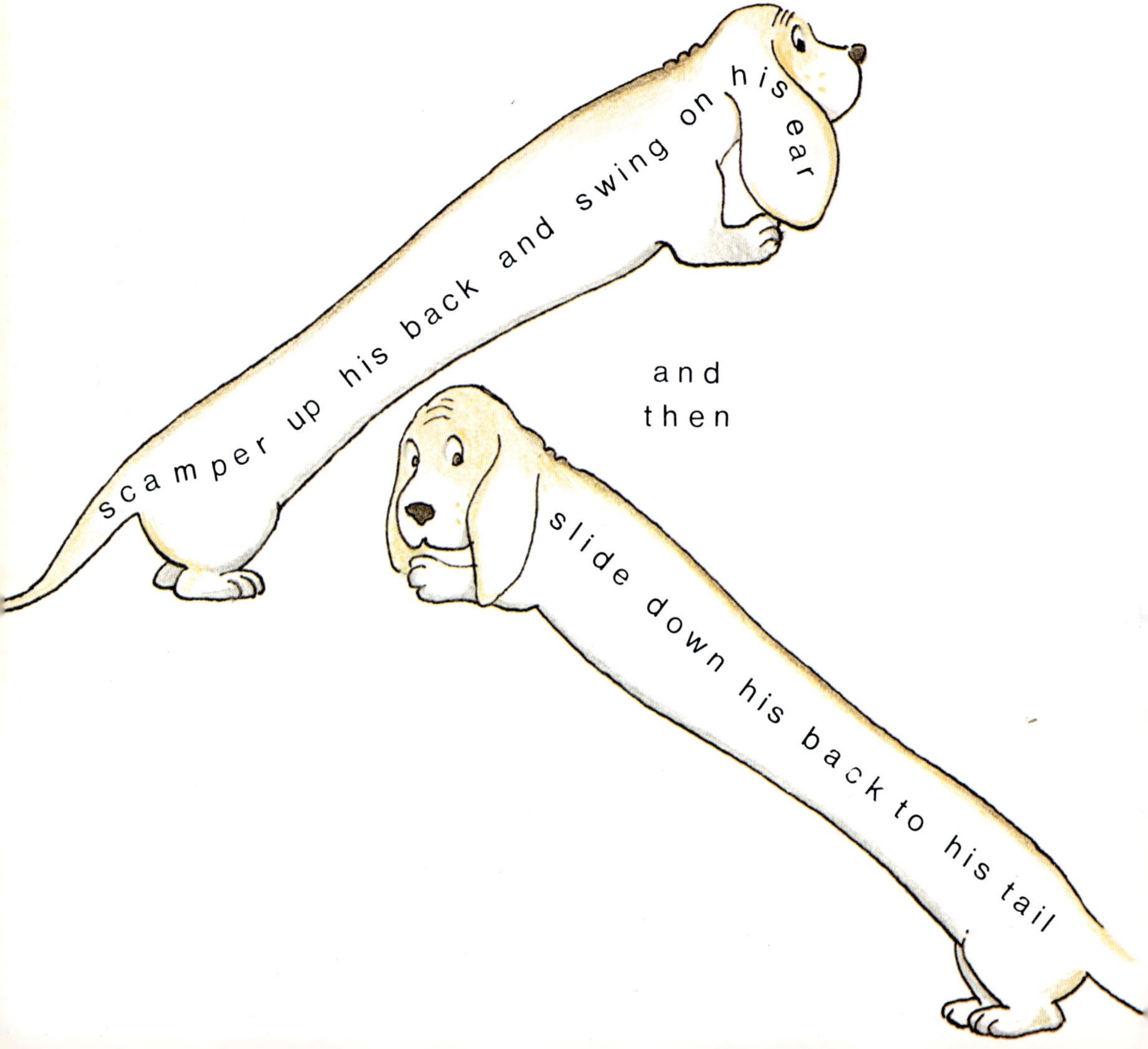

At the end of this game Humph's back was covered with muddy kitten footmarks and when he returned home his mistress had to give him a bath. She filled three bowls with water and

By the time she reached

his front part was

and last his back legs and tail

and when she let him go he shook himself all over and sprinkled the lawn from one end to the other

His mistress was drenched

She managed to catch him again and rinsed him all over in lovely warm water.

Then something funny happened. The rinsing water was so warm that it made Humph shrink. It felt very odd, but there was no doubt about it. As Humph looked behind himself his back legs were getting

He started worrying in case they shrunk right forward and joined on with his front legs. Then he would have been a dog with only

which would have been even more ridiculous than a very, very, very long dog, and much more inconvenient.

HUMPH

He need not have worried. He stopped shrinking at exactly the same size as he had been before the whole adventure started, and, all things considered, although he had enjoyed being famous for a few days as a very, very, very long dog, he is pleased to be just a rather long dog again.

In fact, he is more than pleased.

He is VERY, VERY, VERY, VERY, VERY, VERY, VERY ....

r e l i e v e d!